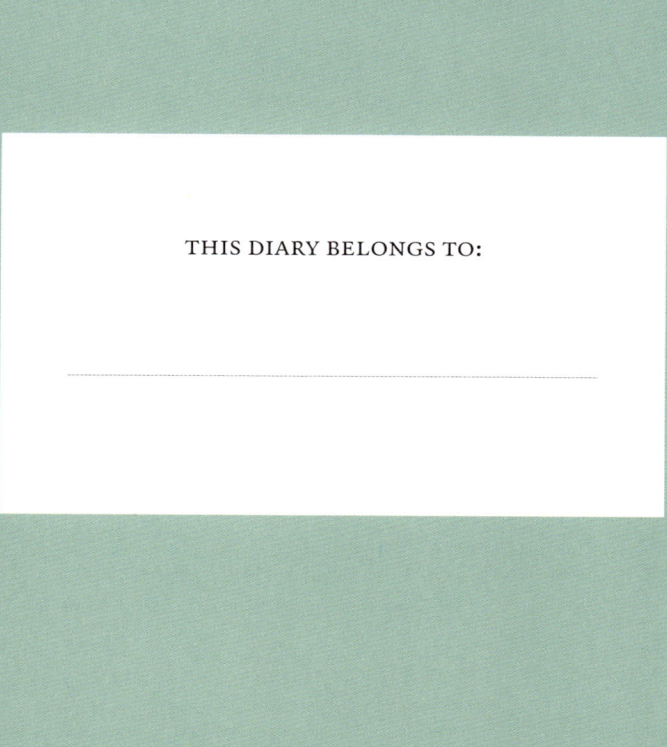

THIS DIARY BELONGS TO:

London Review of Books
28 Little Russell Street, London WC1A 2HN

ISBN 978-1-913465-21-6

Typeset by LRB (London) Ltd
The text is set in Quadraat Pro and Petit Serif

Compiled by Sam Kinchin-Smith
Edited by Jean McNicol
Proofread by Anna Swan
Design by Christopher Thompson
Artwork by Alexander Gorlizki

Printed and bound in Turkey by Imago

Distributed to bookshops by
Profile Books Ltd, 29 Cloth Fair, London EC1A 7JQ

lrb.co.uk

LRB DIARY FOR 2026

# Editorial Note

'Bishop Bonner was of Broadgate hall,' one of the briefest entries in John Aubrey's *Brief Lives* begins:

> When he came to his greatnes, in acknowledgement from whence he had his Rise, he gave to the Kitchin there a great brasse-pott, called Bonners-pott, which was taken away in the Parliament time. Mr. Steevens has shewed the Pott to me, I remember. It was the biggest, perhaps, in Oxford.

That's all we get. And yet doesn't this anecdote – and the implicit message behind it, that this is all you need to know about the notorious persecutor of Protestants under Queen Mary – contain the whole life?

The *LRB Diary for 2026* is our tribute to *Brief Lives* in Aubrey's quatercentenary year. Its premise is that the LRB and Aubrey share a belief in the biographical value of a single, often salacious anecdote. Aubrey's *Brief Lives* began as an index of 55 notable contemporaries. The 55 subjects in this volume, taken from the thousands of biographical pieces contained in the LRB archive, were selected on the basis of several considerations, most of them inspired by Aubrey: there are a handful of figures (Edmond Halley, John Wilmot etc) that Aubrey wrote about; one or two (Isaac Newton, Aphra Behn) that he should have; various recurring preoccupations of the LRB (from Henry James to Wallis Simpson); and a few curveballs, in the manner of Aubrey (who included, among others, Captain Carlo Fantom, 'a Croatian, spake 13 languages . . . hanged for Ravishing').

Everyone included comes from the UK or spent an important part of their life here (again, following Aubrey's criteria) and was born after Aubrey (excepting his own subjects). Each person's entry faces the week containing their birthday, which is marked by a star. This requirement clashed with the ambition to include more LRB obsessions, because their birthdays seem to cluster in certain weeks, such as the one that in 2026 begins on 4 May: Marx, Freud, Blair, not to mention Angela Carter and Alan Bennett. Some subjects are still living (as were some of Aubrey's) and indeed still writing for the LRB.

Three of those included don't get a star: Thomas Wolsey (who is thought to have been born in March 1473, so is allotted the middle week of that month here), and Ignatius Sancho and Francis Williams, who were both born into slavery and whose birthdates weren't recorded or aren't known. You'll find them in the first weeks of 2027. Some of the other birthdates are doubtful: Brigid Brophy wrote a piece for the paper in 1981 about discovering that Behn was probably born on 14 December 1640 (but this was actually the date of her baptism rather than her birth). The change from the Julian to the Gregorian calendar in 1752 also presented challenges. We decided to use Newton's New Style birthdate of 4 January, instead of Christmas Day (his Old Style birthday, as referred to in his excerpt), so we could begin our selection with Aubrey's most famous omission: he loathed Newton. Aubrey also thought Ben Jonson a more important figure than Shakespeare, so we included Jonson and made Wittgenstein, rather than Shakespeare, the subject of the week beginning 20 April.

Many of the extracts have been edited for clarity. A list of links to the original pieces can be found at lrb.me/brieflives

**Sam Kinchin-Smith**

# 2026

## JANUARY

| M | T | W | T | F | S | S |
|---|---|---|---|---|---|---|
| 29 | 30 | 31 | 1 | 2 | 3 | 4 |
| 5 | 6 | 7 | 8 | 9 | 10 | 11 |
| 12 | 13 | 14 | 15 | 16 | 17 | 18 |
| 19 | 20 | 21 | 22 | 23 | 24 | 25 |
| 26 | 27 | 28 | 29 | 30 | 31 | 1 |
| 2 | 3 | 4 | 5 | 6 | 7 | 8 |

## FEBRUARY

| M | T | W | T | F | S | S |
|---|---|---|---|---|---|---|
| 26 | 27 | 28 | 29 | 30 | 31 | 1 |
| 2 | 3 | 4 | 5 | 6 | 7 | 8 |
| 9 | 10 | 11 | 12 | 13 | 14 | 15 |
| 16 | 17 | 18 | 19 | 20 | 21 | 22 |
| 23 | 24 | 25 | 26 | 27 | 28 | 1 |
| 2 | 3 | 4 | 5 | 6 | 7 | 8 |

## MARCH

| M | T | W | T | F | S | S |
|---|---|---|---|---|---|---|
| 23 | 24 | 25 | 26 | 27 | 28 | 1 |
| 2 | 3 | 4 | 5 | 6 | 7 | 8 |
| 9 | 10 | 11 | 12 | 13 | 14 | 15 |
| 16 | 17 | 18 | 19 | 20 | 21 | 22 |
| 23 | 24 | 25 | 26 | 27 | 28 | 29 |
| 30 | 31 | 1 | 2 | 3 | 4 | 5 |

## APRIL

| M | T | W | T | F | S | S |
|---|---|---|---|---|---|---|
| 30 | 31 | 1 | 2 | 3 | 4 | 5 |
| 6 | 7 | 8 | 9 | 10 | 11 | 12 |
| 13 | 14 | 15 | 16 | 17 | 18 | 19 |
| 20 | 21 | 22 | 23 | 24 | 25 | 26 |
| 27 | 28 | 29 | 30 | 1 | 2 | 3 |
| 4 | 5 | 6 | 7 | 8 | 9 | 10 |

## MAY

| M | T | W | T | F | S | S |
|---|---|---|---|---|---|---|
| 27 | 28 | 29 | 30 | 1 | 2 | 3 |
| 4 | 5 | 6 | 7 | 8 | 9 | 10 |
| 11 | 12 | 13 | 14 | 15 | 16 | 17 |
| 18 | 19 | 20 | 21 | 22 | 23 | 24 |
| 25 | 26 | 27 | 28 | 29 | 30 | 31 |
| 1 | 2 | 3 | 4 | 5 | 6 | 7 |

## JUNE

| M | T | W | T | F | S | S |
|---|---|---|---|---|---|---|
| 1 | 2 | 3 | 4 | 5 | 6 | 7 |
| 8 | 9 | 10 | 11 | 12 | 13 | 14 |
| 15 | 16 | 17 | 18 | 19 | 20 | 21 |
| 22 | 23 | 24 | 25 | 26 | 27 | 28 |
| 29 | 30 | 1 | 2 | 3 | 4 | 5 |
| 6 | 7 | 8 | 9 | 10 | 11 | 12 |

## JULY

| M | T | W | T | F | S | S |
|---|---|---|---|---|---|---|
| 29 | 30 | 1 | 2 | 3 | 4 | 5 |
| 6 | 7 | 8 | 9 | 10 | 11 | 12 |
| 13 | 14 | 15 | 16 | 17 | 18 | 19 |
| 20 | 21 | 22 | 23 | 24 | 25 | 26 |
| 27 | 28 | 29 | 30 | 31 | 1 | 2 |
| 3 | 4 | 5 | 6 | 7 | 8 | 9 |

## AUGUST

| M | T | W | T | F | S | S |
|---|---|---|---|---|---|---|
| 27 | 28 | 29 | 30 | 31 | 1 | 2 |
| 3 | 4 | 5 | 6 | 7 | 8 | 9 |
| 10 | 11 | 12 | 13 | 14 | 15 | 16 |
| 17 | 18 | 19 | 20 | 21 | 22 | 23 |
| 24 | 25 | 26 | 27 | 28 | 29 | 30 |
| 31 | 1 | 2 | 3 | 4 | 5 | 6 |

## SEPTEMBER

| M | T | W | T | F | S | S |
|---|---|---|---|---|---|---|
| 31 | 1 | 2 | 3 | 4 | 5 | 6 |
| 7 | 8 | 9 | 10 | 11 | 12 | 13 |
| 14 | 15 | 16 | 17 | 18 | 19 | 20 |
| 21 | 22 | 23 | 24 | 25 | 26 | 27 |
| 28 | 29 | 30 | 1 | 2 | 3 | 4 |
| 5 | 6 | 7 | 8 | 9 | 10 | 11 |

## OCTOBER

| M | T | W | T | F | S | S |
|---|---|---|---|---|---|---|
| 28 | 29 | 30 | 1 | 2 | 3 | 4 |
| 5 | 6 | 7 | 8 | 9 | 10 | 11 |
| 12 | 13 | 14 | 15 | 16 | 17 | 18 |
| 19 | 20 | 21 | 22 | 23 | 24 | 25 |
| 26 | 27 | 28 | 29 | 30 | 31 | 1 |
| 2 | 3 | 4 | 5 | 6 | 7 | 8 |

## NOVEMBER

| M | T | W | T | F | S | S |
|---|---|---|---|---|---|---|
| 26 | 27 | 28 | 29 | 30 | 31 | 1 |
| 2 | 3 | 4 | 5 | 6 | 7 | 8 |
| 9 | 10 | 11 | 12 | 13 | 14 | 15 |
| 16 | 17 | 18 | 19 | 20 | 21 | 22 |
| 23 | 24 | 25 | 26 | 27 | 28 | 29 |
| 30 | 1 | 2 | 3 | 4 | 5 | 6 |

## DECEMBER

| M | T | W | T | F | S | S |
|---|---|---|---|---|---|---|
| 30 | 1 | 2 | 3 | 4 | 5 | 6 |
| 7 | 8 | 9 | 10 | 11 | 12 | 13 |
| 14 | 15 | 16 | 17 | 18 | 19 | 20 |
| 21 | 22 | 23 | 24 | 25 | 26 | 27 |
| 28 | 29 | 30 | 31 | 1 | 2 | 3 |
| 4 | 5 | 6 | 7 | 8 | 9 | 10 |

## JANUARY

| M | T | W | T | F | S | S |
|---|---|---|---|---|---|---|
| 28 | 29 | 30 | 31 | 1 | 2 | 3 |
| 4 | 5 | 6 | 7 | 8 | 9 | 10 |
| 11 | 12 | 13 | 14 | 15 | 16 | 17 |
| 18 | 19 | 20 | 21 | 22 | 23 | 24 |
| 25 | 26 | 27 | 28 | 29 | 30 | 31 |
| 1 | 2 | 3 | 4 | 5 | 6 | 7 |

## FEBRUARY

| M | T | W | T | F | S | S |
|---|---|---|---|---|---|---|
| 1 | 2 | 3 | 4 | 5 | 6 | 7 |
| 8 | 9 | 10 | 11 | 12 | 13 | 14 |
| 15 | 16 | 17 | 18 | 19 | 20 | 21 |
| 22 | 23 | 24 | 25 | 26 | 27 | 28 |
| 1 | 2 | 3 | 4 | 5 | 6 | 7 |
| 8 | 9 | 10 | 11 | 12 | 13 | 14 |

## MARCH

| M | T | W | T | F | S | S |
|---|---|---|---|---|---|---|
| 1 | 2 | 3 | 4 | 5 | 6 | 7 |
| 8 | 9 | 10 | 11 | 12 | 13 | 14 |
| 15 | 16 | 17 | 18 | 19 | 20 | 21 |
| 22 | 23 | 24 | 25 | 26 | 27 | 28 |
| 29 | 30 | 31 | 1 | 2 | 3 | 4 |
| 5 | 6 | 7 | 8 | 9 | 10 | 11 |

## APRIL

| M | T | W | T | F | S | S |
|---|---|---|---|---|---|---|
| 29 | 30 | 31 | 1 | 2 | 3 | 4 |
| 5 | 6 | 7 | 8 | 9 | 10 | 11 |
| 12 | 13 | 14 | 15 | 16 | 17 | 18 |
| 19 | 20 | 21 | 22 | 23 | 24 | 25 |
| 26 | 27 | 28 | 29 | 30 | 1 | 2 |
| 3 | 4 | 5 | 6 | 7 | 8 | 9 |

## MAY

| M | T | W | T | F | S | S |
|---|---|---|---|---|---|---|
| 26 | 27 | 28 | 29 | 30 | 1 | 2 |
| 3 | 4 | 5 | 6 | 7 | 8 | 9 |
| 10 | 11 | 12 | 13 | 14 | 15 | 16 |
| 17 | 18 | 19 | 20 | 21 | 22 | 23 |
| 24 | 25 | 26 | 27 | 28 | 29 | 30 |
| 31 | 1 | 2 | 3 | 4 | 5 | 6 |

## JUNE

| M | T | W | T | F | S | S |
|---|---|---|---|---|---|---|
| 31 | 1 | 2 | 3 | 4 | 5 | 6 |
| 7 | 8 | 9 | 10 | 11 | 12 | 13 |
| 14 | 15 | 16 | 17 | 18 | 19 | 20 |
| 21 | 22 | 23 | 24 | 25 | 26 | 27 |
| 28 | 29 | 30 | 1 | 2 | 3 | 4 |
| 5 | 6 | 7 | 8 | 9 | 10 | 11 |

## JULY

| M | T | W | T | F | S | S |
|---|---|---|---|---|---|---|
| 28 | 29 | 30 | 1 | 2 | 3 | 4 |
| 5 | 6 | 7 | 8 | 9 | 10 | 11 |
| 12 | 13 | 14 | 15 | 16 | 17 | 18 |
| 19 | 20 | 21 | 22 | 23 | 24 | 25 |
| 26 | 27 | 28 | 29 | 30 | 31 | 1 |
| 2 | 3 | 4 | 5 | 6 | 7 | 8 |

## AUGUST

| M | T | W | T | F | S | S |
|---|---|---|---|---|---|---|
| 26 | 27 | 28 | 29 | 30 | 31 | 1 |
| 2 | 3 | 4 | 5 | 6 | 7 | 8 |
| 9 | 10 | 11 | 12 | 13 | 14 | 15 |
| 16 | 17 | 18 | 19 | 20 | 21 | 22 |
| 23 | 24 | 25 | 26 | 27 | 28 | 29 |
| 30 | 31 | 1 | 2 | 3 | 4 | 5 |

## SEPTEMBER

| M | T | W | T | F | S | S |
|---|---|---|---|---|---|---|
| 30 | 31 | 1 | 2 | 3 | 4 | 5 |
| 6 | 7 | 8 | 9 | 10 | 11 | 12 |
| 13 | 14 | 15 | 16 | 17 | 18 | 19 |
| 20 | 21 | 22 | 23 | 24 | 25 | 26 |
| 27 | 28 | 29 | 30 | 1 | 2 | 3 |
| 4 | 5 | 6 | 7 | 8 | 9 | 10 |

## OCTOBER

| M | T | W | T | F | S | S |
|---|---|---|---|---|---|---|
| 27 | 28 | 29 | 30 | 1 | 2 | 3 |
| 4 | 5 | 6 | 7 | 8 | 9 | 10 |
| 11 | 12 | 13 | 14 | 15 | 16 | 17 |
| 18 | 19 | 20 | 21 | 22 | 23 | 24 |
| 25 | 26 | 27 | 28 | 29 | 30 | 31 |
| 1 | 2 | 3 | 4 | 5 | 6 | 7 |

## NOVEMBER

| M | T | W | T | F | S | S |
|---|---|---|---|---|---|---|
| 1 | 2 | 3 | 4 | 5 | 6 | 7 |
| 8 | 9 | 10 | 11 | 12 | 13 | 14 |
| 15 | 16 | 17 | 18 | 19 | 20 | 21 |
| 22 | 23 | 24 | 25 | 26 | 27 | 28 |
| 29 | 30 | 1 | 2 | 3 | 4 | 5 |
| 6 | 7 | 8 | 9 | 10 | 11 | 12 |

## DECEMBER

| M | T | W | T | F | S | S |
|---|---|---|---|---|---|---|
| 29 | 30 | 1 | 2 | 3 | 4 | 5 |
| 6 | 7 | 8 | 9 | 10 | 11 | 12 |
| 13 | 14 | 15 | 16 | 17 | 18 | 19 |
| 20 | 21 | 22 | 23 | 24 | 25 | 26 |
| 27 | 28 | 29 | 30 | 31 | 1 | 2 |
| 3 | 4 | 5 | 6 | 7 | 8 | 9 |

# Isaac Newton

## CHRISTOPHER HILL

Far and away the best psychohistorian of Newton is Frank Manuel. He emphasises Newton's childhood – the undersized posthumous son of a Lincolnshire yeoman, whose mother (a gentleman's daughter) remarried when he was three and left him in the care of his grandmother. On the death of his step-father, when Newton was eleven, they were reunited. Until her death in 1679, when Isaac was 36, his mother remained almost the only human being who was close to him. Newton's annus mirabilis, 1665-66, in which he discovered the calculus, the nature of white light and the theory of gravity, was spent at her house; the apple fell in her garden.

Manuel's theory, put forward with judicious tentativeness, is that Isaac's early separation from his mother left a wound that never healed. This accounts for his withdrawn personality, his secrecy and evasiveness, his insistence on absolute loyalty in his dependants and his rejection of them when they fell short by his exacting standards. Newton's fierce hatreds of rivals are assoc-iated with childish desires to murder the stepfather who had robbed him of his mother. No earthly father figure could replace the father he had never known. Newton, born on Christmas Day, regarded himself as in some special sense the favoured son of a Father in heaven who was all-powerful and all-demanding.

Vol. 2 No. 17 · 4 September 1980

29  Monday

30  Tuesday

31  Wednesday

1  Thursday                                                    NEW YEAR'S DAY

2  Friday                                                      2ND JANUARY (SCOT)

3  Saturday                              4  Sunday ★

# David Bowie

## IAN PENMAN

He left spaces for his followers: not just the hierarchy of star-
dom and fandom but a strange, astute, uncanny folding of one
into the other. From album to album there was a strange, light,
almost mocking dialectic: he taught us to be critics of our own
enthusiasms. He was 'post' and 'meta' and playfully 'iconic', before such terms had any real popular currency. July 1972: blue
guitar, red boots, jumpsuit made of cushion covers from a bad
mescaline trip, orange hair, a Klieg-light nimbus around his
ghost-train head. A big crooked grin like he's having the best
possible time, like he has just sold the waiting world a truly
irresponsible dare, his arm curling around the guitarist Mick
Ronson. 'But he thinks he'd blow our minds!' And he did. One
reason for that blown fuse was that Bowie had already worked
out that the best way to put across a serious point was to stage it
as an almost luridly OTT showbiz scene. You have to remember
that *Top of The Pops* was it. There was no pop media at large, only
three channels: everyone in the country was eating their tea
and watching the same flicker of sound and vision. And here
was this flirtatious pop-art revelation, all under the disbelieving
eyes of everyone's parents: a cosy family teatime – then wham
bang! Did you see that! What on earth was going on there? Then
he was gone.

Vol. 39 No. 1 · 5 January 2017

5 Monday

6 Tuesday

7 Wednesday

8 Thursday ★

9 Friday

10 Saturday

11 Sunday

# David Lloyd George

## SUSAN PEDERSEN

Imagine you are hired, fresh out of college at the age of 24, as tutor to the teenage daughter of the chancellor of the exchequer. His wife is away in the country much of the time; he wanders about 11 Downing Street in his carpet slippers. He looks at you a lot, and brushes up against you in the hallway when he passes. You know he has a terrible reputation, but if you are honest with yourself you have to admit you quite fancy him. The tension in the house becomes palpable, and after some months the chancellor pops the question. Will you be his secretary, on the understanding that he gets to sleep with you as well? He won't leave his wife for you, he won't destroy his career, but as the confidante and adviser of one of the government's brightest stars, you'll share a good slice of his life.

What woman would agree to this unequal bargain? Well, early in 1913, when Lloyd George was the chancellor making the proposal, Frances Stevenson, the daughter of a Scottish accountant and his part-French, part-Italian wife, did so. I can see why, and it isn't just that I've always had a soft spot for Lloyd George, who was a flesh and blood human being, and not one of those conscience-laden stick-figures in morning coats that the Edwardian Liberal Party produced in such numbers. It's also that so few real opportunities were open to a young woman with a head for politics in that era.

Vol. 29 No. 2 · 25 January 2007

12 Monday

13 Tuesday

14 Wednesday

15 Thursday

16 Friday

17 Saturday ★                    18 Sunday

# Virginia Woolf

## JACQUELINE ROSE

One of the strangest things Virginia Woolf ever did was to travel with her husband, Leonard, to Germany for part of their annual holiday in April 1935. The vigour of German antisemitism was by this point clear and Hitler's power and at least some of his worst intentions towards Britain were recorded by Woolf in her diaries ('There is some reason I suppose to expect that Oxford Street will be flooded with poison gas one of these days'). But it wasn't uncharacteristic of her to make light of danger. Although in many ways her life seems closeted, guarding its safety till the last, Virginia Woolf took risks with herself. Five years later, caught in an air raid with Ben Nicolson, who sagely threw himself to the ground, she stood still and lifted her arms to the sky. More sinisterly, caught in the middle of a flag-waving crowd of Nazi supporters shouting 'Heil Hitler' in the course of the trip to Germany, she had raised her arm in salute.

As with all moments of excess in the life and writing of Virginia Woolf, these stories present us with a question. What might lead someone, in a position of real danger, to identify with, stretch out – yearn – towards the aggressor? What might lead someone to seem passionately to covet what they most fear?

Vol. 19 No. 2 · 23 January 1997

19  Monday

20  Tuesday

21  Wednesday

22  Thursday

23  Friday

24  Saturday

25  Sunday ★

# Paula Rego

## GABY WOOD

Paula Rego and Victor Willing met at a house party, sometime around the coronation of Elizabeth II. He was behind her on the stairs, and guided her into a bedroom. 'Take down your knickers,' he said. It didn't occur to Rego to refuse. 'I was a virgin, so you can imagine the mess,' she told their son. 'He could at least have hailed me a taxi.' After a number of back-street abortions, she decided to keep her next baby, then kept two more. She moved back to Portugal. Willing eventually left his wife and joined her.

Willing was diagnosed with multiple sclerosis in 1966. For the rest of that decade and all of the next, Rego felt she was 'treading water'. In the early 1980s she experimented with large, unbridled paintings of almost comic-book violence, featuring a recurring character, Red Monkey. A few years later, after she'd seen the work of the so-called outsider artist Henry Darger, she riffed on his schoolgirl characters, the 'Vivian girls', in frantically populated acrylics. As Willing's health deteriorated, she acquired focus: the cartoon figures crystallised into a series of paintings of an oversized young girl looking after a large dog. The girl is caring, taunting, playful and dangerous by turns, the balance of power firmly in her favour. She feeds the dog, lifts her skirt for him, adjusts his collar, shaves him with a lethal-looking razorblade. The dog, Rego never hesitated to say, was Willing.

Vol. 43 No. 19 · 7 October 2021

26  Monday  ★

27  Tuesday

28  Wednesday

29  Thursday

30  Friday

31  Saturday                    1  Sunday

# Simone Weil

## TORIL MOI

In August 1936, Simone Weil crossed the Spanish border and made her way to Barcelona. There she managed to join a group of international volunteers in the small town of Pina de Ebro. Noticing her short-sightedness, her comrades at first refused to give her a weapon. But she demanded so vociferously to be allowed to carry a rifle like everyone else that they relented (though they prudently stayed out of range). One morning, less than two weeks after her arrival, she failed to see a vat of boiling oil on the ground and stepped into it, suffering terrible burns. After a few days, transportation was found to get her back to Barcelona. If her parents had not been waiting there, to provide treatment, food and rest, she might well have died. Towards the end of September, they finally persuaded her to return to France with them.

This became a recurring pattern. Weil acted on conviction, always with great courage and absolute determination. But in the background, her parents were ready to drop everything to make sure that she survived her attempts at living out her ideals. Gustave Thibon, the editor of one of her most popular books, *Gravity and Grace*, thought that their 'constant care . . . put off the inevitable outcome'. The Weils themselves were perfectly aware of their role. 'If you ever have a daughter,' her mother said to the poet Jean Tortel, 'pray to God she won't be a saint.'

Vol. 43 No. 13 · 1 July 2021

2  Monday

3  Tuesday  ★

4  Wednesday

5  Thursday

6  Friday

7  Saturday

8  Sunday

# Thomas Malthus

## OLIVER CUSSEN

Malthus was born in 1766, the sixth of seven children in a prosperous family. His education was indulgent and progressive, thanks to a father obsessed with Rousseau and a series of reform-minded tutors who remarked on the contrarian temperament of 'Don Roberto', his love of 'fighting for fighting's sake'. He studied mathematics and natural philosophy at Cambridge, and decided at the age of twenty to take orders and find 'a retired living in the country'. In 1789, as revolutionaries in Paris abolished feudalism and issued the Declaration of the Rights of Man, Malthus was appointed to a curacy near Dorking. He moved back in with his parents and settled into a humdrum rustic lifestyle: recycled sermons for Surrey parishioners, the occasional holiday in the Lake District. But the enthusiasm with which contemporaries celebrated the events in France eventually reawakened the intellectual ambitions of his youth, as well as an adolescent passion for picking fights with the Enlightenment. The revolutionaries in France had stirred up 'disgusting passions of fear, cruelty, malice, revenge, ambition, madness and folly, as would have disgraced the most savage nation in the most barbarous age'. The task Malthus set himself in writing the *Essay on Population* was to prove the existence of the natural law that radicals had ignored at such great cost.

Vol. 46 No. 18 · 26 September 2024

9 Monday

10 Tuesday

11 Wednesday

12 Thursday

13 Friday ★

14 Saturday                         15 Sunday

# W.H. Auden

## ALAN BENNETT

In April 1939, W.H. Auden, Christopher Isherwood and Louis MacNeice gave a reading at the Keynote Club in Manhattan. Chester Kallman and another Brooklyn College student, Walter James Miller, were in the audience, with Kallman sitting in the front row giving the two international pederasts the glad eye. Afterwards he and Miller went backstage. Miller was tall, blond, Anglo-Saxon and (a friend who was not a friend) heterosexual. Predictably it was to the unavailable Miller that Auden took a fancy, leaving it to the more realistic Isherwood to chat up the all too available Kallman. Miller had written an article for the college literary magazine and Auden expressed a desire to read it. Twenty years later, when he was professor of poetry at Oxford, Auden's desires were still being expressed in the same guileless way: undergraduate poets asked round to read him their verse in the hope that one thing might lead to another. However, on the day appointed it was not Miller who turned up but Kallman. Isherwood was in the next room when Auden came through and said: 'It's the wrong blond.' The rest is history. Or literature. Or the history of literature. Or maybe just gossip. And on that score anathema to Auden himself, who, wanting no biography, would have been appalled to read this blow-by-blow account of his sex life.

Vol. 7 No. 9 · 23 May 1985

16 Monday

17 Tuesday

18 Wednesday

19 Thursday

20 Friday

21 Saturday ★

22 Sunday

# Elizabeth Taylor

## BEE WILSON

Taylor's parents were both Americans, but they were living in London when she was born. Her godfather was a rich Conservative MP called Victor Cazalet who helped the family live a more upper-middle-class existence than they would otherwise have been able to afford. When she was three, Cazalet gave Elizabeth a pony called Betty. Riding Betty prepared her for the role of Velvet in *National Velvet*, but it was also, as Kate Andersen Brower writes, 'the only time she was allowed to be a child'. Her mother, Sara, had aspirations for her daughter and enrolled her in the Vacani School of Dance. Aged just three and a half, Taylor performed in a white tutu and butterfly wings at the Queen's Hall in front of Princess Elizabeth. At the end, all the other dancers left while Taylor sat alone in the middle of the stage. Sara remembered her own pleasure at that moment: 'I knew that day that there would come a time when she would want to follow in my footsteps.'

The outbreak of the Second World War set Taylor on a path to Hollywood. In April 1939, Cazalet told her father to send his wife and children to the US, for safety. It was only a couple of years before the nine-year-old Elizabeth signed her first movie contract, with Universal. The contract was cancelled after a year, with the casting director complaining that 'her eyes are too old; she doesn't have the face of a kid.'

Vol. 38 No. 9 · 5 May 2016

23 Monday

24 Tuesday

25 Wednesday

26 Thursday

27 Friday ★

28 Saturday

1 Sunday

# Elizabeth Barrett Browning

## ALETHEA HAYTER

Elizabeth Barrett was a 'teazer par excellence', as she herself said: she could not resist an occasional deliberate misunderstanding of Browning's words, and her little flourishes of feigned indignation sometimes frightened him into portentous apologies, so that she had eventually to suggest that – like the earliest painters, who when they painted a tree used to write under it 'This is a tree' – she ought to write under her sallies, 'This is a jest,' to prevent him from taking them too seriously. One of their finest exchanges was over the morality of duelling, on which they had a serious disagreement. Browning first mentioned in a letter, and partly justified, the practice of duelling; they discussed it on one of his visits soon afterwards; a day later she wrote vehemently condemning it as a crime which no outdated notion of 'honour' could justify, and worked herself up into writing that if Browning fought a duel, 'I would just *call in the police*, though you were to throw me out of the window afterwards.' Browning was alarmed, and wrote an immense letter of reasoned arguments and instances justifying duelling in certain circumstances, but pleading for her forgiveness. In her reply, she sadly maintained her disagreement, and he gave way: 'YOU ARE RIGHT and I am wrong.' She disclaimed didacticism, and the subsequent reiterations of their worship of each other were all the warmer for the battle.

Vol. 11 No. 7 · 30 March 1989

2  Monday

3  Tuesday

4  Wednesday

5  Thursday

6  Friday  ★

7  Saturday

8  Sunday

# John Aubrey

## ADAM SMYTH

The enthusiasm that courses through all his writings is John Aubrey's sociability, his delight in the atoms of news whirling around him. We could call him a gossip, but he was more benign than that; Anthony Wood described him as 'roving and magotieheaded, and sometimes little better than crased', but Aubrey's information-gathering had at its heart a desire to preserve a present that was fading even as it occurred: he was haunted, like a Shakespeare sonnet, by the life that passes without memorial. Always, according to Anthony Powell, 'trying to draw the chill of his childhood's loneliness from his bones', Aubrey thrived in an Oxford that was (in his own words) 'facetious and diverting', a place of anecdote and conversation. He lived in coffee houses; he scribbled as people talked; he watched his friends rise and fall; he travelled miles to see them. 'It seems to me that between the years 1649 and 1670, I was never off horseback.' The flipside of Aubrey being, in William Poole's words, 'politically tone-deaf' is a ranging inclusivity in his social relations: John Dryden, Andrew Marvell, Edmund Waller, Thomas Hobbes, John Locke, John Milton, Wenceslaus Hollar. As Kate Bennett writes in the introduction to her superb new edition of *Brief Lives*, 'we may be able to hear, through him, the 17th century talking to and about itself.'

Vol. 37 No. 19 · 8 October 2015

9  Monday

10  Tuesday

11  Wednesday

12  Thursday ★

13  Friday

14  Saturday

15  Sunday

# Thomas Wolsey

## BLAIR WORDEN

What then of the traditional charges against Wolsey? Did he
not aim to become pope, an ambition bound to conflict with
Henry VIII's diplomatic and ecclesiastical priorities, and did he
not milk and bully the English Church to his own financial ends?
By no means, says Peter Gwyn. His foreign policy and his man-
agement of the Church were directed solely to the nation's interests. But did not Wolsey, by concentrating in his person so many
of the abuses that produced the anti-clericalism of the age,
make the Church vulnerable to the Reformation? Far from it.
Pre-Reformation anti-clericalism has existed only in the minds
of Protestant historians, who have judged Wolsey by anachron-
istic standards. Yes, he practised nepotism and lived opulently
and ostentatiously, but that was the way the Church's leaders
were expected to behave. If he had 'no great knowledge of the
Bible', and if he is 'most unlikely' to have 'ever had a religious
vocation', then those defects too, if defects they were, were un-
exceptional and therefore unimportant. They did not impair his
plans to reform the Church. He aimed to close down some of
the decayed monasteries, and to reorganise the dioceses, so as
to fortify the Church against the Lutheran threat. If his plans for
reforms were limited, it was because fundamental change was
unnecessary. If they were not fully implemented, it was because
he prudently avoided confrontation.

Vol. 12 No. 19 · 11 October 1990

16 Monday

17 Tuesday

ST PATRICK'S DAY

18 Wednesday

19 Thursday

20 Friday

21 Saturday

22 Sunday

# William Morris

## MICHAEL LEDGER-LOMAS

Like the Persian carpets Morris admired, his poems interlaced Troy, Byzantium and Arabia. He compared the difficulties of writing his next multi-layered long poem, *Love Is Enough* (1872), to lining up the repeats in a tapestry. The risk of weaving verse is that you end up turning it out by the yard: *The Earthly Paradise* eventually ran to 42,000 lines. By describing himself in its preface as the 'idle singer of an empty day', Morris encouraged people to dismiss his entire corpus as whiffle. That is unfair, but extracts suggest how easily his poetry could become a mellifluous soporific: the 'hapless lover's dull shame sinks/ Away sometimes in day-dreams, and he thinks/No more of yesterday's disgrace and foil.' The disgrace was personal. By the time he was writing the poem, the Red House was sold and his wife, Jane, was involved with Dante Gabriel Rossetti, who called her Lucrezia Borgia and documented their affair in blazing portraits. Morris compounded everyone's suffering by deciding to let the lovely Kelmscott Manor as their country bolthole. Rossetti installed himself there and poisoned it with his drugged paranoia. Perhaps the romance of marriage would have dwindled anyway, even without this skunk in the orchard.

Vol. 47 No. 8 · 8 May 2025

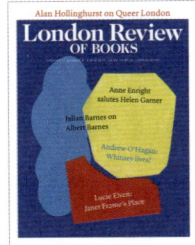

23 Monday

24 Tuesday ★

25 Wednesday

26 Thursday

27 Friday

28 Saturday

29 Sunday

# John Wilmot

## TERRY EAGLETON

There was a streak of madness about the Earl of Rochester, a perverse, Wilde-like impulse to self-destruction. Rather as Wilde appeared to be courting disaster, so Rochester seemed to do his best to enrage the monarch on whom his fortunes depended. When Charles asked to see a satirical poem that was circulating at court, Rochester handed him instead a vituperative lampoon of the king he had written himself. Whether he did this by accident or design is unclear. Perhaps it was a Freudian parapraxis, consciously accidental but unconsciously intended. In any case, Charles was furious, Rochester was banished from the court yet again and his various pensions and salaries suspended. He was reinstated some time later, only to be pitched out once more when he threw himself in a drunken rage on a phallic-shaped sundial dear to the king's heart crying, 'What! Do you stand here to fuck time?' and slashed it to pieces with his rapier. It was said to be the most elaborate and expensive instrument of its kind in Western Europe. Astonishingly, he survived this episode too, since Charles had need of his political support.

As the syphilis addled his brain he grew odder and odder. He disguised himself for a few months as a gorgeously attired Italian physician, Alexander Bendo, and set up shop in a London street offering cures for scurvy, back pain, bad teeth, obesity, consumption and a number of other afflictions.

Vol. 36 No. 20 · 23 October 2014

30  Monday

31  Tuesday

1  Wednesday ★

2  Thursday

3  Friday                                              GOOD FRIDAY

4  Saturday                    5  Sunday              EASTER SUNDAY

# Leonora Carrington

## ALICE SPAWLS

In Paris she completed her first major self-portrait, *Inn of the Dawn Horse* (1937). A wild-haired Leonora dressed in riding clothes sits in a room with her hyena familiar; behind her on the wall hangs a rocking horse, and through the window a second horse gallops. The painting features many of the themes she would return to in later works: anthropomorphism, wild-haired women, ambiguous interior spaces, the horse as freedom and sexuality. 'A horse gets mixed up with one's body,' she said, 'it gives energy and power.'

In 1938 Carrington and Max Ernst moved to a farmhouse in Provence, decorating it with bird and horse talismans to keep away disapproving parents and warring Surrealists, as well as Ernst's wife. War broke out and Ernst was interned first by the French, and then by the Germans. Carrington was taken to Madrid by friends, where she began to suffer delusions – she had been starving herself for weeks – and was put into an asylum. Here her story becomes increasingly strange. She was given the drug Cardiazol, which induced terrible fits, before being rescued, possibly by her nanny, possibly in a submarine (her father was friends with Churchill). Chaperoned to Lisbon to board a boat for South Africa, she escaped through a window and went to the Mexican embassy, where Renato Leduc, whom she knew through Picasso, offered to marry her so she could get to America.

Vol. 37 No. 8 · 23 April 2015

6  Monday  ★                          EASTER MONDAY (NOT SCOT)

7  Tuesday

8  Wednesday

9  Thursday

10  Friday

11  Saturday                    12  Sunday

# Henry James

## COLM TÓIBÍN

Henry James's letters home can be read as sly and manipulative, but he wrote them for a good reason. He had been haphazardly educated by his parents to prepare him for nothing; they had kept him away from America for some of the crucial years of his adolescence, so his circle of friends, as these letters show, was extremely limited, many of his associates being also friends of the family. His parents had effectively banished their two younger sons, Wilkie and Bob, in whom they never had any great interest. They had made Alice, their only daughter, an invalid. In other words, the parents of Henry James had to be watched very carefully. Escaping them was an imperative. If illness, real or imaginary, kept them at bay, distracted them from doing damage, then it was a small price to pay. Had Henry James not managed them so carefully, he might never have got away. Or might never have managed the parting with such ease, such a lack of rancour, making clear to them once he had left for good that he loved them and missed them, and basking in the glow of their love and approval, but from afar.

Managing his family with slow doses of deceit was also useful to James as a novelist for whom secrecy and subterfuge was a great theme. Manipulating others, bending them with subtlety towards your will, sweetly deceiving them, was something his characters would do with considerable skill.

Vol. 30 No. 1 · 3 January 2008

13 Monday

14 Tuesday

15 Wednesday ★

16 Thursday

17 Friday

18 Saturday                                    19 Sunday

# Ludwig Wittgenstein

## JONATHAN RÉE

In November 1910 a Jewish engineer at Victoria University in Manchester obtained a patent for a new kind of aeronautical propeller. He was just 21, and well on the way to achieving his childhood dream of becoming the greatest aviator since Orville and Wilbur Wright. But he hesitated. He had been reading Gottlob Frege and Bertrand Russell in his spare time, and believed that their inquiries into the foundations of logic heralded a revolution even more exciting than the invention of powered flight. He wanted to be part of it if he could. The following year he was knocking on Russell's door at Trinity College, Cambridge, and the great man was sufficiently impressed to let him enrol at once as an undergraduate student. After a while Russell regretted his decision, writing in letters to his friend Ottoline Morrell that his 'German engineer' was a 'fool' who kept pestering him with stupid questions. But then he changed his mind, saying that the 'ferocious German (who is an Austrian I find)' appeared to be 'really intelligent' after all.

A few weeks more and Russell was completely won over, treating Ludwig Wittgenstein as a brilliant colleague rather than a tiresome student, and as living proof that 'making machines' is a better preparation for work in philosophy than a British classical education.

Vol. 41 No. 22 · 21 November 2019

20  Monday

21  Tuesday

22  Wednesday

23  Thursday

24  Friday

25  Saturday                              26  Sunday ★

# Mary Wollstonecraft

## FRANCESCA WADE

Wollstonecraft's first vindication of the rights of woman was the rescue of her sister Eliza from a violent husband. She also founded a school, but was determined to support herself by writing. In this she was helped by the publisher Joseph Johnson, whose three o'clock salons – known as 'a Menagerie of Live Authors' – introduced her to the work of Thomas Paine, William Blake, Benjamin Franklin and Joseph Priestley. Johnson taught her to 'offend, alienate and strenuously disagree' in her unsigned pieces for his monthly *Analytical Review*; with his encouragement she wrote *A Vindication of the Rights of Men* (1790) in response to Burke's attack on the French Revolution. Critics, predictably, were outraged (Horace Walpole called her a 'hyena in petticoats'). She responded with *A Vindication of the Rights of Woman* (1792). Inspired by European political theory, and reacting to the weak heroines of Rousseau's novels as well as her own experience, she criticises kings and domestic tyrants, and argues that a society which keeps women as 'alluring mistresses' and treats them as 'a kind of subordinate beings, and not as a part of the human species' degrades men and women alike. 'Every day,' Virginia Woolf wrote of Wollstonecraft, 'she made theories by which life should be lived; and every day she came smack against the rock of other people's prejudices.'

Vol. 37 No. 19 · 8 October 2015

27 Monday ★

28 Tuesday

29 Wednesday

30 Thursday

1 Friday

2 Saturday

3 Sunday

# Sigmund Freud

## MIKKEL BORCH-JACOBSEN

'Was Freud a liar?' Ever since Frank Cioffi had the audacity to
ask this question in 1973, it has continued to rock the world of
psychoanalysis. Till then, things had been so simple. Children
of the 'Freudian century', we had all learned to venerate in Sig-
mund Freud a man of 'absolute honesty' and 'flawless integrity',
as his loyal biographer Ernest Jones called him. It was his
passion for truth that enabled him to confront the demons of
his own unconscious and to lift the multisecular repression
that weighed on sexuality, despite the 'resistance' of his patients
and the attacks of his colleagues. It was this scientific probity,
too, which made him acknowledge his error about the fantastic
'scenes' of incest and sexual molestation that his patients had
been bringing to him, despite the stinging professional setback
this represented for him. In Freud, science coincided with the
moral fibre of the scientist, whose edifying biography we never
tired of reading: Anna O.'s miraculous 'talking cure', the break
with Josef Breuer regarding sexuality, the abandonment of the
'seduction theory', the tearing away from the transference on
Wilhelm Fliess, the stoicism in the face of his colleagues' attacks.

It is a nice story, but we now know it to be nothing but a
vast legend. One after another, historians of psychoanalysis have
come forward to show us that things did not happen in the way
Freud and his authorised biographers told us.

Vol. 22 No. 8 · 13 April 2000

4  Monday                                    EARLY MAY BANK HOLIDAY

5  Tuesday

6  Wednesday ★

7  Thursday

8  Friday

9  Saturday                    10  Sunday

# Mary Wortley Montagu

## RUTH BERNARD YEAZELL

There was always more than one Lady Mary, and more than one accounted for her final two decades of exile on the Continent. If she was once again a tourist, she was now also a tourist attraction: 'I verily beleive,' Lady Mary wrote from Venice, 'if one of the Pyramids of Ægypt had travell'd, it could not have been more follow'd.' At Avignon, she had only to admire an ancient tower for the town council to vote her its lifetime use as a belvedere; at Gottolengo, it was all she could do to prevent the citizens from setting up a marble statue of her, book in hand, in the town square.

She had left England unhappy with both her children, mysteriously alienated from her daughter (who was now Lady Bute), and despairing of her son. Though time and distance did little for the lying and dissolute Edward, they served to turn Lady Bute into the beloved recipient of some lively remarks on contemporary fiction and a number of memorable letters on the education of women. It was to this 'Dear Child' that the mother addressed her bemused irony when the publication of a partly misattributed poem threatened to renew old scandals: 'I thank God Witches are out of Fashion, or I should expect to have it depos'd by several credible wittnesses that I had been seen flying through the Air on a broomstick etc.'

Vol. 21 No. 11 · 27 May 1999

11  Monday

12  Tuesday

13  Wednesday

14  Thursday

15  Friday ★

16  Saturday                                    17  Sunday

# W.G. Sebald

## MICHAEL WOOD

Sebald's deep preoccupation is with what his character Jacques Austerlitz calls 'the marks of pain', psychological and physical, in human and other animals. These marks are indelible, and for some people unforgettable. For others, though, they are all too deniable, and resolutely covered up. A notable instance of the second reaction is the silence that refuses to recognise there was ever any noise. It may start in a kind of innocence. Carole Angier describes the moment in 1962 when Sebald and his schoolmates were shown Billy Wilder's documentary about the concentration camps. 'Afterwards nothing was said. No one knew how to react, so they just went off to a football match.' The continuation of the silence becomes a conspiracy. Sebald thought things would change when he went to university, but 'the recent past was as carefully avoided in the classroom as it had been at home.' 'You were surrounded by dissembling old fascists,' he later said. Angier suggests there were two major silences for Sebald: about the Holocaust and about the Allied bombings of German cities, both examples of the human appetite for the destruction of others. Of course we don't call this an appetite, but that is part of the silence, and one of Sebald's most powerful myths – those places where 'fact and fiction are, so to speak, inseparably linked together' – suggests that every ambitious construction is designed to arrive at its own ruin.

Vol. 44 No. 1 · 6 January 2022

18  Monday  ★

19  Tuesday

20  Wednesday

21  Thursday

22  Friday

23  Saturday                                              24  Sunday

# Ian Fleming

## CHRISTIAN LORENTZEN

Fleming the inveterate shagger had finally decided to marry Ann, widow of Lord O'Neill and until recently wife of Esmond, 2nd Viscount Rothermere, owner of the *Daily Mail*. In January 1952, with prenuptial jitters, he sat down in Goldeneye, his bungalow in Jamaica, and wrote *Casino Royale* at a pace of two thousand words each morning. He would enact the same ritual annually until his death from a heart attack in 1964. Until near the end, when Fleming at last sorted out the film rights for 007, money worries were never far from his mind.

When Truman Capote pays a visit, Fleming writes to Ann: 'Can you imagine a more incongruous playmate for me?' He seems happiest discussing technical details, as when a gun expert, Geoffrey Boothroyd, wrote to say that Bond shouldn't be packing a Beretta .25. The Walther PPK was Boothroyd's suggestion; 'if possible,' he added, 'don't have anything to do with silencers.' Fleming replied: 'I sympathise with you about not liking silencers, but the trouble is that there are occasions when they are essential to Bond's work.'

Vol. 37 No. 23 · 3 December 2015

25  Monday

26  Tuesday

27  Wednesday

28  Thursday ★

29  Friday

30  Saturday                    31  Sunday

# George III

## ALAN BENNETT

When I began to read about George III, it was the first systematic historical work I'd done in twenty years. I found that his rehabilitation had proceeded apace. No longer the ogre, he had grown altogether more kindly, wiser even, and in his attachment to his people and his vision of the nation over and above the vagaries of politics, he had come to seem a forerunner of a monarch of the present day. But it was a joke that made me think of writing about him. He had an equerry, Colonel Manners, who, bringing him his dinner one day, discovered the king had hidden under the sofa. A Jeeves before his time, Manners imperturbably laid a place for His Majesty on the carpet and put down the plate. He was retiring discreetly when the king said (still *sous bergère*), 'That was very good . . . Manners.' The pun was thought to signal a further stage in the king's recovery. The anecdote hasn't found its way into my play, but it did make me think that George III might be fun to write about.

From a dramatist's point of view, it is obviously useful if the king's malady was a toxic condition, traceable to a metabolic disturbance rather than due to schizophrenia or manic depression. Thus afflicted, he becomes the victim of his doctors and a tragic hero. How sympathetic this would make him to the audience I had not realised until the previews of the play.

Vol. 14 No. 2 · 30 January 1992

1 Monday

2 Tuesday

3 Wednesday

4 Thursday ★

5 Friday

6 Saturday                          7 Sunday

# Ben Jonson

## TERENCE HAWKES

Jonson's interest in digestion and excretion and their relationship to literary activity has attracted previous scholars, and Edmund Wilson's essay of 1948, 'Morose Ben Jonson', is perhaps
the best-known example of what it can lead to. Anxious to pin
the desperate label 'anal neurotic' on the poet, Wilson duly list-
ed orderliness, parsimony and obstinacy, together with a fix-
ation on symbolic substitutes for faeces, such as money, as
major characteristics of the man and his work. His prim conclus-
ion that 'when he is dirty, he is, unlike Shakespeare, sometimes
disgusting to such a degree that he makes one sympathetic with
the Puritans in their efforts to clean up the theatre' helped to
construct Jonson as what Bruce Thomas Boehrer terms 'one of
the two great anal basket cases of English literary history' – the
other being Swift. What Wilson – and Eliot before him – failed
to notice is that Jonson's interest in bodily functions, his un-
relenting pursuit of the links between the alimentary and the
literary, his preoccupation with eating, evacuation, vomiting
and the all-too-human stench that these disseminate are less
shortcomings in need of explanation than dimensions of an art
whose true contours we still fail accurately to discern. At the very
least they measure the extent to which his writings, like those
of Shakespeare, draw vital sustenance from 'a network of tent-
acular roots reaching down to the deepest terrors and desires'.

Vol. 20 No. 10 · 21 May 1998

8  Monday

9  Tuesday

10  Wednesday

11  Thursday ★

12  Friday

13  Saturday                                    14  Sunday

# Wallis Simpson

## PAUL FOOT

Charles Higham's is an important book. But there is a great deal wrong with it. It is no good inventing (or guessing at) Wallis Simpson's sexual education in the brothels of Shanghai or for that matter entering the royal bedchamber to speculate about what exactly went on there. There are times – far too many of them – when bald assertions are not backed by the evidence they need; the notes and the index are a disgrace; and Higham's biographical method, piling incident on incident and referring only to the day and the month, continually loses the thread of the narrative.

But these are really niggles. Gossip is a dangerous commodity, but no biography worth its salt could survive without it. The plain fact is that, for all its weaknesses, the book is enthralling from first to last and for one central reason. It exposes both its main subject and her royal catch, not as the dim-witted, self-obsessed lovers who have been pickled for posterity, but as nasty, determined fascists who wanted to preside over a 'new social order' which would do away for ever with all pretence at democracy and consign all opposition to the Holocaust.

Vol. 10 No. 16 · 15 September 1988

15  Monday

16  Tuesday

17  Wednesday

18  Thursday

19  Friday  ★

20  Saturday                              21  Sunday

# George Orwell

## IAN HAMILTON

If Orwell were alive today, he would surely be one of those disputants who likes to have 'the figures here in front of me', or close to hand. From Wigan onwards, he was forever making lists. He kept a Fishing Log when he went fishing, an Eggs Laid Log when he kept chickens, and he could not read a newspaper without measuring the distribution of column inches: ads v. news. He divided the books in his library into Books Borrowed/ Books Bought/Books Reviewed. His notes to his literary executor are remarkably meticulous, detailing the publishing histories of his writings, including individual essays. Over the years, he put together a large collection of political pamphlets and was always on the lookout for new items. He was also pretty keen on gardening and carpentry. Orwell the nerd?

All the same, some of Orwell's lists are rather moving, especially when we remember how ill he was much of the time, and how absurdly busy – as a writer. Maybe these tabulations were for him a means of keeping the lid on an unstable temper. Or were they his way of readying himself for some imminent, Orwellian tribunal (you asked to see my papers, here they are)? Whatever the impulse, they can from time to time induce a sense of pathos. Was Orwell never, so to speak, off-duty? Was there no social problem that he could think of as, well, not his problem?

Vol. 20 No. 21 · 29 October 1998

22  Monday

23  Tuesday

24  Wednesday

25  Thursday  ★

26  Friday

27  Saturday                    28  Sunday

# Princess Diana

## JENNY DISKI

Ten years on, with so many more screens and pages clogged with celebrity, and the broadsheets gone overtly tabloid, it isn't entirely obvious what fascinated people so about Diana Windsor, née Spencer, the uneducated, O-level-free daughter of an ancient house, former nanny, Sloane, clothes horse, playgirl, campaigner, therapist addict. Take the bright lights away and you have a regular messy divorce, friends taking sides, money, adultery, using the kids. The only remarkable thing was that he left her for an older woman. The rest is pedestrian, and the fact that it was a royal divorce doesn't quite make up for the dullness of most of the characters involved. It was, perhaps, Princess Diana's contradictions that kept the interest alive. She spent £3000 a week on grooming and hugged lepers. She secretly visited centres for the homeless, taking her sons with her to ensure they learned about privilege, and issued an angry public statement when a tabloid picture showed a suggestion of cellulite on her thighs. But scrutinise the first 36 years of anyone's life and you will find no end of contradictions (with the possible exception of Paris Hilton's). It was just that for a brief period Diana had more and grander opportunities for contradictory behaviour than most of us. This might be what celebrity obsession is: watching and waiting for them to get all the usual things wrong, but on a monstrous scale.

Vol. 29 No. 15 · 2 August 2007

13 Monday ★  BATTLE OF THE BOYNE SUBSTITUTE DAY (NI)

14 Tuesday

15 Wednesday

16 Thursday

17 Friday

18 Saturday  19 Sunday

# Masud Khan

## WYNNE GODLEY

We hardly ever spoke of my childhood. Khan preferred, he said, to 'work out of' the material which was thrown up by contemporary experiences. Everything of significance that had happened in the past could be reinterpreted in terms of what was happening now. This gave him a licence to interfere actively, judgmentally and with extraordinary cruelty in every aspect of my daily life. We entered a long period of painful stasis. 'When is something going to happen?' I would ask and he would reply: 'I wonder too when something is going to happen. I have exhausted' – these were his exact words – '*every manoeuvre that I know*. You are a tiresome and disappointing man.'

Khan liked it when I moved up through the Treasury ranks, greatly overestimating the importance and significance of the positions which I held. Meanwhile he began increasingly to fill the sessions with tales about his own social life in London or, occasionally, New York. The stories were not good ones. Many were obscene and many were flat, but there was one feature common to every one of them: Khan had got the better of someone. He had rescued Mike Nichols from a man with a fierce dog in New York. He had fought physically with Peter O'Toole, using a broken bottle. He had got the overflow from his lavatory to pour a jet of water onto the head of a woman who was making her car hoot in the street below.

Vol. 23 No. 4 · 22 February 2001

20  Monday

21  Tuesday  ★

22  Wednesday

23  Thursday

24  Friday

25  Saturday

26  Sunday

# Emily Brontë

## JOHN BAYLEY

She *was* Heathcliff: not a man exactly, but a concept of self outside man or woman, 'a chainless soul' trapped in an unspecifiable body, a challenge that still hypnotises our concepts of gender, role and personality. This lack of conditioned and conventional gender must also explain the fascination she has exercised over so many people, after her late Victorian apotheosis, when they could respond to 'passion's splendour' without identifying it in any specific sexual context. But the real context is actually a very down-to-earth one: a hatred of the body, its weakness, greed and depravity, as if it were a horrid child inside which was trapped a free consciousness. Emily towards the end sought unexalted remedies, not only starving but purging herself, clearly hooked on the state of bodilessness described and longed for in the poems. Nothing could have suited better the parsonage's resident population of tubercle bacilli. Her father had almost died of it once, after the death from TB of his wife and two elder daughters, and had kept his throat and chin ever since swathed in cravats and what he hoped were prophylactic bandages. Big and tough as she was, Emily could probably have continued to resist the latent infection, as tiny Charlotte did, if she had fed herself properly. As it was, weakened by fasting and aperients, she was the first of the remaining sisters to go.

Vol. 12 No. 24 · 20 December 1990

27  Monday

28  Tuesday

29  Wednesday

30  Thursday ★

31  Friday

1  Saturday

2  Sunday

# Philip Larkin

## MARK FORD

Larkin carefully and deliberately avoided allowing his lodgings in Wellington, in Leicester, in Belfast, and finally in Hull, to be homely. In his poetry he often trumpeted his evasion of all sense of belonging, as in 'Places, Loved Ones': 'No, I have never found/ The place where I could say/This is my proper ground,/Here I shall stay.' ('Touché,' Larkin responded when his staff at the Brynmor Jones Library in Hull gave him a card inscribed with exactly these lines at a lunch to commemorate his 25th anniversary as head librarian there.) Not until 1974, when the university sold the Pearson Park flat (where Larkin had lived for eighteen years, even though it was supposed to be a temporary lodging for newly arrived lecturers), did he grudgingly acquire what might be called a home, purchasing an ugly red-brick 1950s house in a Hull suburb. Was it any coincidence that in the decade he spent there he completed only a couple of poems (the melancholy self-elegy 'Aubade' and the savage 'Love Again')? Larkin may not have swaggered the nut-strewn roads, or crouched in the fo'c'sle, stubbly with goodness (as he comically figured the life of the happy-go-lucky wanderer in 'Poetry of Departures'), but by maintaining a sense of provisionality in his various rented attics, and by keeping his successive lovers at arm's length, he managed to preserve not only the sense of freedom that was necessary for his poems, but the connection to his mother that nourished them.

Vol. 41 No. 12 · 20 June 2019

3  Monday

4  Tuesday

5  Wednesday

6  Thursday

7  Friday

8  Saturday

9  Sunday ★

# Letitia Elizabeth Landon

## CYNTHIA LAWFORD

When 'L.E.L.', at the age of nineteen, first caught the public's attention, readers of the weekly *Literary Gazette* (most of its 1822 and 1823 issues contained her verses) wondered if her poetry, especially the rambling, blank-verse 'Poetic Sketches' of beautiful women destroyed by their affections for absent men, was written at speed, inspired by passion. In *The Improvisatrice*, which went to six editions, L.E.L. played up to her public image, claiming that 'It was not song that taught me love,/But it was love that taught me song.'

Those who met her or heard the London gossip knew that Landon flouted convention in ways that would have dismayed many of her admirers. She didn't live in Brompton with her upper-middle-class (though poor) parents, but in Chelsea. After her father died in 1824, the money she made by her writing supported both her mother and her brother. Yet she appeared quite carefree, adopting romantic dress and seeming to pay little regard to how immodest or unfashionable her attire – or behaviour – might appear. Invited by ladies of rank to lend their parties the sparkle of her celebrity, she liked to cause a stir by scorning the lachrymose sentiments of her verse and laughing at the notion that she could ever become attached to a single man. She also liked to make jokes at the expense of fellow guests: wit was no more approved of in young ladies than sexual cravings.

Vol. 22 No. 18 · 21 September 2000

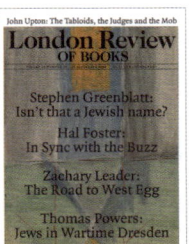

10  Monday

11  Tuesday

12  Wednesday

13  Thursday

14  Friday  ★

15  Saturday

16  Sunday

# V.S. Naipaul

## PAUL THEROUX

Out of Naipaul's shadow, I saw his contradictions clearly, and I am still seeing them – his divided self, his many moods. In good health he was superb; after a bad night, or in a depressive frame of mind, he was a doomsayer. He could be flatly mistaken about writers. The cruelty in his remarks was unjustifiable. He was often wrong. People are not wicked for being overweight or ill-favoured. It is not true that the oppressed are always to be feared. The writing of Nabokov or Updike may not be a window-pane, but it is often brilliant. Joyce and Beckett are inimitable. Africa has not returned to bush, though many of its people are badly governed, and exploited by outside interests. Offering someone a second chance is a humane act. And no matter how much encouragement writers who are starting out receive, they are still forced to make their own way, scribble-scribble.

One of Naipaul's generalisations about writers was in a magazine story about John Steinbeck: 'A writer is in the end not his books, but his myth. And that myth is in the keeping of others.' Naipaul is not a myth to me. Now and then someone tells me they've read him and offers an opinion, and I don't recognise the man they're describing.

Vol. 44 No. 4 · 24 February 2022

17  Monday  ★

18  Tuesday

19  Wednesday

20  Thursday

21  Friday

22  Saturday

23  Sunday

# Jean Rhys

## MARY-KAY WILMERS

At the age of six a photograph had been taken of her: she looked very pretty in a new white dress. Three years later, she realised 'with dismay that I wasn't like it any longer': 'It was the first time I was aware of time, change and the longing for the past. I was nine years of age.'

Jean Rhys didn't really change much after the age of nine. A sense of loss, which was primarily aesthetic, and a consequent sense of being at a loss, seem to have dominated her life – or the record she wished to give of her life – as they dominate her writing. Their circumstances and their resourcefulness may vary a little, but almost all Jean Rhys's heroines, both in her novels and in her short stories, suffer from a similar incapacity to wake up from a dream. They know this about themselves, but the world seems to them too harsh and they lack the 'nous' to deal with it: 'Take my advice and grow another skin or two . . . before it's too late,' a young man remarks to the nous-less heroine of 'Till September Petronella'. Jean Rhys's mother, who didn't like her very much, worried about her ability to look after herself: 'I can't imagine what will happen if you don't learn to behave more like other people.'

Vol. 2 No. 3 · 21 February 1980

24 Monday ★

25 Tuesday

26 Wednesday

27 Thursday

28 Friday

29 Saturday          30 Sunday

# Duleep Singh

## ERIC STOKES

He bought Elveden in Suffolk, with its splendid sporting estate, and entertained the Prince of Wales and the great peers in lavish style. Yet when he found that his allowance could not sustain his grand way of life and that for all her importunity, the queen could not persuade her ministers to raise the allowance, he slowly began to repent him of the surrender of his Indian personality, his religion and his sovereign rank. Losing all sense of reality, he renounced Christianity, revived extinct claims to land and jewels, and threatened to stir up political trouble in India. The queen rightly thought that he had gone off his head. When he attempted to return to India, he was detained at Aden; when he 'defected' to Russia and was received by the tsar, it soon became evident that St Petersburg also did not think him an asset worth the charge of upkeep. He was forced to eat humble pie and return to his English paymasters. The remaining brief period of his troubled existence was spent wandering among Continental spas and the Riviera resorts. Victoria's compassion for a fallen king and personal protégé rose superior to racial or political differences. On a private visit to Grasse in 1891 she invited Duleep to meet her. When the now obese invalid, half-paralysed from a stroke, broke violently into sobbing, Victoria 'stroked and held his hand, and he became calm and said: "Pray excuse me and forgive me my faults."'

Vol. 2 No. 7 · 17 April 1980

31 Monday

SUMMER BANK HOLIDAY (NOT SCOT)

1 Tuesday

2 Wednesday

3 Thursday

4 Friday

5 Saturday

6 Sunday ★

# H.D.

## MAUREEN N. MCLANE

Hilda Doolittle was born in Bethlehem, Pennsylvania in 1886, the only daughter and second child of the second marriage of Charles Doolittle, professor of astronomy and mathematics and Civil War veteran, and Helen Wolle, from a Moravian background, whose family had long been resident in the area. (Moravian Christians were heirs to the dissident, pietistic, communal ethos of the 15th-century reformer Jan Hus of Bohemia.) H.D.'s mythopoetic inclinations were later fed by such details: the Bethlehem birth, a sense of prophetic giftedness handed down the maternal line, an inheritance she also characterised as 'Eleusinian' as against the 'Athenian' (embodied by her father and older half-brother, also an astronomer). The Eleusinian Mysteries became a key motif in her work, which repeatedly stages scenes of initiation and decipherment: erotic, mystical, esoteric, divinely feminine. As a writer and an analysand, H.D. understood herself to be shaping and sustaining her 'own LEGEND'. She was quite at home with Keats's idea that a 'life of any worth is a continual allegory – and very few eyes can see the Mystery of life.' The terms she often used instead of 'allegory' were 'myth', 'legend', 'signet', 'cryptogram' and 'hieroglyph'. There was a lot of Pennsylvania shrewdness shining through the mythic mist. 'Sylvania. I was born here. People ought to think before they call a place Sylvania.'

Vol. 45 No. 3 · 2 February 2023

7 Monday

8 Tuesday

9 Wednesday

10 Thursday ★

11 Friday

12 Saturday

13 Sunday

# Agatha Christie

## JOHN LANCHESTER

Absence, the things that aren't said, and aren't necessarily there even in the unsaid, is very important to Agatha Christie. Her autobiographical writing is startlingly lacking in introspection, so much so that it makes you wonder at the nature of the psychological absence inside Christie, the space and silence where certain kinds of conversation with herself might be expected to take place. *Come, Tell Me How You Live*, a memoir about her life with her second husband, the archaeologist Max Mallowan, is a serious contender for the least revealing autobiographical book ever written, strongly rivalled by her *Autobiography*, which does at least contain some factual details from her childhood. It is in character that the most famous thing which ever happened to Christie was that she ran away and disappeared for a few days, a classic fugue which ended with her being found living under an assumed name in a hotel in Harrogate. Perhaps her entire being, her inner life, was a kind of absence, a variety of fugue.

What there was instead of an interest in character and selfhood and complex psychology – as opposed to the psychology of types – was an interest in form.

Vol. 40 No. 24 · 20 December 2018

14 Monday

15 Tuesday ★

16 Wednesday

17 Thursday

18 Friday

19 Saturday

20 Sunday

# Diane Abbott

## FLORENCE SUTCLIFFE-BRAITHWAITE

Diane Abbott's mother eventually left her father, unable to deal with his controlling behaviour and rage. Abbott has arrived at a hard-won and painful understanding of the way her father's daily experience of racism affected him. She narrates good-humouredly the response of an older friend, Ros Howells, to her pregnancy: not wanting Abbott to be a single mother as well as the only Black female MP, Howells brokered a marriage with the child's father. It didn't last, and Abbott describes the complications she encountered while parenting as a parliamentarian, including the furore over her son's schooling. She knew when she decided to send him to the fee-paying City of London School that it would be controversial; for years she had campaigned about racism and discrimination in the state school system, but it seemed the media 'had no interest in Black children in general, though they were only too interested in this one child'. Her son, at home with a babysitter one night, heard a slew of criticism of her on an LBC phone-in and rang in himself. 'I will always feel guilty and sad,' Abbott writes, 'that my 11-year-old son felt he had to wade in to defend his mother.' She still attracts a staggering amount of bile. During the 2017 election campaign, Amnesty tracked abusive tweets sent to 177 women MPs; Abbott was the target of 45 per cent of all these tweets, many of them virulently racist.

Vol. 46 No. 21 · 7 November 2024

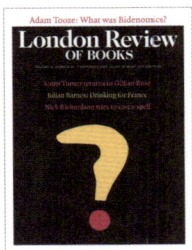

21  Monday

22  Tuesday

23  Wednesday

24  Thursday

25  Friday

26  Saturday                    27  Sunday ★

# Elizabeth Gaskell

## DINAH BIRCH

Gaskell's father was an accomplished writer who died without having quite fulfilled his early promise. Her brother also had wanted to write, and had not been able to do so. One of his last letters to her contains a moment of encouragement that might have lingered in her mind: 'You have really made a very pretty story of Captain Barton – it would almost make the foundation of a novel.' Years later, her first novel was about a family called Barton. Gaskell was prompted to write *Mary Barton* by the death of her only son, a tragedy that could well have revived her earlier grief for the loss of her brother. Charlotte Brontë, who became a close friend and the subject of one of Gaskell's best books, also lost her mother while still very young and was left to the care of an aunt. She, too, had a father with frustrated literary hopes, and a brother whose aspirations to write terminated in a pitiably early death. Though Victorian women had to contend with many disadvantages, to be born a man was no guarantee of success. The autonomy that produced the novels of Gaskell and Brontë was shadowed and sanctioned by the unwritten fiction of dead brothers.

Vol. 19 No. 19 · 2 October 1997

28  Monday

29  Tuesday ★

30  Wednesday

1  Thursday

2  Friday

3  Saturday                    4  Sunday

# John Lennon

## JEREMY HARDING

It's clear that this clever man profited from his relationship with Yoko Ono, who served his purposes in serving her own. Under her guidance, Lennon became both a public solipsist and something of a radical – affirming the paramount value of being John before going on to adopt the campaigning postures of the 1970s: anti-war, anti-consumerism, anti-Nixon, anti-clericalism, a brief bout of workerism, 'power to the people' and so on. It was rickety stuff, but for most of the time he meant it, and within a few years of his liaison with Yoko, he had graduated from the knowing boy of the 1960s to the naive man-child we associate with his last years. 'Imagine' – his transnational anthem of 1971 – is typical of the new universalist peering out through smoked-glass spectacles. Direct, fantastical, awash with grandeur and schmaltz, and apparently harmless, it might nowadays have been commissioned for a Vodafone ad. Even so, it must have had an edge to it when Lennon performed it at a benefit for the relatives of inmates killed by police after the Attica State Prison riot in 1971 and it was BBC policy, nearly twenty years later, to keep it off the air for the duration of the Gulf War.

Vol. 23 No. 1 · 4 January 2001

5  Monday

6  Tuesday

7  Wednesday

8  Thursday

9  Friday  ★

10  Saturday                    11  Sunday

# Margaret Thatcher

## CHRISTOPHER HITCHENS

At once we were in an argument. Of Joshua Nkomo I remember her saying: 'I think Joshua is absolutely *sweet*.' That was the least of our disagreements. On one point of fact, too abstruse to detail here, I was right (as it happens) and she was wrong. But she *would* not concede this and so, rather than be a bore, I gave her the point and made a slight bow of acknowledgment. She pierced me with a glance. 'Bow lower,' she commanded. With what I thought was an insouciant look, I bowed a little lower. 'No, no – *much* lower!' A silence had fallen over our group. I stooped lower, with an odd sense of having lost all independent volition. Having arranged matters to her entire satisfaction, she produced from behind her back a rolled-up parliamentary order paper and struck – no, she thwacked – me on the behind. I reattained the perpendicular with some difficulty. 'Naughty boy,' she sang out over her shoulder as she flounced away. Nothing that happened to the country in the next dozen years surprised me in the least.

Actually, I was surprised by a few things. But whenever I read of the humiliation of some over-mighty cabinet colleague – Geoffrey Howe, say, or Jim Prior or John Moore or Francis Pym – I could picture the scene only too well.

Vol. 16 No. 20 · 20 October 1994

12　Monday

13　Tuesday ★

14　Wednesday

15　Thursday

16　Friday

17　Saturday　　　　　　　　　　18　Sunday

# Tariq Ali

## ANDY BECKETT

Connoisseurship, conviviality, exotic locations, encounters and debates with other worldly individuals: left-wing politics as presented here is often far from the grind of cold picket lines or meetings in draughty halls. Back in London, Ali is invited to *Private Eye* lunches and talks to fellow Hampstead and Highgate lefties about 'new additions to our libraries' of political first editions. Some of his other allies in the capital are more surprising. Shortly after 9/11, he gets a phone call from 'a friend belonging to the upper reaches of Saudi society'. Over lunch, she tells him that her family in Riyadh are thrilled at 'what we did' to the US, supposedly Saudi Arabia's close ally. In 1983, he talks to Indira Gandhi, India's then prime minister, while researching a book about her family. 'After the formal interview,' he writes, 'Mrs Gandhi turned to me: "Now my turn to ask some questions. I read your new book [*Can Pakistan Survive?*]. You know these [Pakistani] generals and how they think and operate. I'm being told by my people here that Pakistan is preparing a surprise attack on us in Kashmir. What do you think?"'

Connectedness, confidence and dissent run in Ali's family. One of his grandfathers was 'the elected premier of the Punjab'. His father was an anti-imperialist, a leftist, a fiercely independent newspaper and magazine editor, and 'the All-India backstroke champion' before his part of Punjab became part of Pakistan.

Vol. 47 No. 3 · 20 February 2025

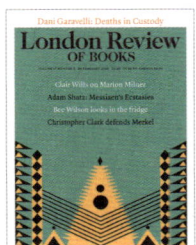

19  Monday

20  Tuesday

21  Wednesday ★

22  Thursday

23  Friday

24  Saturday

25  Sunday

# Sylvia Plath

## JOANNA BIGGS

In Devon, aged thirty and with her husband gone, Plath rode horses and took up smoking. She learned how to keep the coal stove going all day – something Ted had never mastered. She did the paperwork, dug the garden, took the bins out. She had lost twenty pounds, but began cooking and eating again. 'Ted may be a genius,' she wrote to her mother, 'but I'm an intelligence.' She took up tarot, wondered about Connemara or Spain to escape another winter. Women rallied round: her midwife found a 22-year-old trainee nurse to take care of the children while Sylvia wrote, late poppies and cornflowers on her desk. Ruth Fainlight wrote supportively from Tangier, accepting the dedication of 'Elm', and her family and friends in Massachusetts wrote and sent money and things for the children. But she refused to let her mother rescue her: 'I must make a life as fast as I can,' she wrote, 'all my own.' Olive Higgins Prouty sent a cheque and suggested she go shopping. In Winkleigh, Sylvia went to the hairdresser, getting a more fashionable fringe cut in but keeping the long braid she curled around her crown. She went to Jaeger – 'it is my shop,' she told Prouty – and bought a camel suit and sweater, a blue and black tweed skirt, a green cardigan, black sweater and red wool skirt, with earrings, hair clasp and bracelet made of pewter to match. 'My new independence delights me.' She planned to raise the hems of all her old clothes.

Vol. 40 No. 24 · 20 December 2018

26 Monday

27 Tuesday ★

28 Wednesday

29 Thursday

30 Friday

31 Saturday · 1 Sunday

# Edmond Halley

## STEVEN SHAPIN

Joined for all time on the title page of the Book that Made the Modern World are Isaac Newton (who wrote the *Principia Mathematica*) and Samuel Pepys (who, as president of the Royal Society, licensed it to be printed). It is one of the oddest couples in the history of thought: the man who, as a late 17th-century Cambridge student was heard to say, had 'writt a book that neither he nor any body else understands' and one of the multitude who understood scarcely a word of it; the wholly other and the all-too-human. Turn the page and the odd couple is joined by a third, for here appears the name of the astronomer Edmond Halley – the midwife to modernity. Halley it was who pressed Newton to write the book, who saw it through the press and corrected the sheets, who paid for its publication out of his own pocket, and who prepared a précis for personal presentation to the king – one of the earliest scientific soundbites. Halley was alter ego to the wholly other. He understood both the significance of Newton's celestial dynamics and the emotional dynamics of Newton's tortured soul.

If you want to understand the culture that joined Newton and Pepys on the *Principia*'s title page, your best bet is understanding Edmond Halley. For it was Halley's life that linked the intellectually transcendent with the mundanely practical, the life of solitary scholarship with pressing Crown concerns.

Vol. 20 No. 13 · 2 July 1998

2 Monday

3 Tuesday

4 Wednesday

5 Thursday

6 Friday

7 Saturday

8 Sunday ★

# Charlotte Mew

## PENELOPE FITZGERALD

Death, in Charlotte Mew's dreams and metaphors, had been an identification with the sky at sunset – 'when you are burned quite through you die' – or a walk down a dim street where, at lamplighting time, she would meet herself, or a rambling sailor waiting for her on every quay. These images, projected at random from the buried self, create the poem in their own right. They are romantic images; but death was also 'the whole dreadful heap' which she had witnessed often enough, and the time when she would not have to think any more, or even be.

'I mean to go through the door without fear,' she had also written. She had always assumed that she would know when the right moment had come. Just before one o'clock on 24 March she went out for a few minutes and bought a bottle of lysol, a disinfectant which contained enough creosote to be a corrosive poison. She poured half the bottleful into a glass on the washstand and drank it. At the inquest (the reporters did not get her name right and she was described as 'Miss New, a writer of verse') she was said to have been found lying fully clothed on the bed, 'conscious and muttering to herself'. Dr Cowan and Miss Lutch entered the room together. The doctor administered olive oil, and Charlotte came round sufficiently to say: 'Don't keep me, let me go.' Then she lost consciousness, and died at three o'clock that afternoon.

Vol. 24 No. 10 · 23 May 2002

9  Monday

10  Tuesday

11  Wednesday

12  Thursday

13  Friday

14  Saturday

15  Sunday ★

# Benjamin Britten

## NICHOLAS SPICE

Like one of George Crabbe's peculiar Suffolk coastal flowers, or a weed forcing its way through concrete, Britten's genius was tough and indomitable: drawing sustenance from wherever it could, pushing towards the light by whatever involuted route it could find, and in the course of time bolting over a huge area of English musical culture with its strange, unwholesome blooms. Not the least wonderful aspect of this prodigious musical plant was the way it colonised the preserves of the English middle class. By the time he had become Lord Britten – the only English composer ever so to be ennobled – Benjamin Britten was English music, as far as the middle-class establishment was concerned. His following among the frightfully nice extended to the queen and the queen mother. That delightful Mr Britten, dear sweet Ben, with his ambassadorial accent and the demeanour of the head of an Oxbridge college, and his music about sexual frustration, sadism and despair. When one looks back on Britten's life, it is hard to tell who was co-opting whom. My own sense is that Britten had the last laugh. In the Belvedere Museum in Vienna, I once observed an old lady, buried in furs and hung about with priceless jewellery, peer impassively through a lorgnette at Egon Schiele's drawings of women masturbating. The rituals of the Aldeburgh festival played out a similar game of double standards.

Vol. 15 No. 3 · 11 February 1993

16  Monday

17  Tuesday

18  Wednesday

19  Thursday

20  Friday

21  Saturday                              22  Sunday ★

# William Blake

## IAIN SINCLAIR

There is no single Blake. Not any longer, not once the envelope of identity had been laid aside (his stone slab in Bunhill Fields, close to the memorials for Defoe and Bunyan, is a sentimental prompt and not a marker for his bones). It is not known where he is buried, or where Catherine Blake, his father, mother and brothers are to be found. It is our weakness to insist on having a mossy tablet to represent memory, to provide a focus for our pilgrimages. Poets, from the body of work, from the surviving texts, create the Blake that best suits their purposes. Michael McClure discovers a form of energy, muscular and swift, a poetic prescription with which he can 'write the body'. The Californian Blake. Allen Ginsberg, famously, heard Blake's voice while lying on his bed masturbating in Harlem: a voice 'with all the infinite tenderness and mortal gravity of a living Creator speaking to his son'. The two poets, debating their experiences, realised that they had 'two different Blakes'. McClure spoke of it in an interview with Jerry Aronson: 'Allen has a Blake who is a Blake of prophesy, a Blake who speaks out against the dark satanic mills. My Blake is a Blake of body and of vision. Blake was such a powerful, such a great being that it's possible for every one of us to have an entirely different Blake.' The act of biography is therefore undesirable, if not openly treacherous, a defiance of the poet's will.

Vol. 18 No. 4 · 22 February 1996

23  Monday

24  Tuesday

25  Wednesday

26  Thursday

27  Friday

28  Saturday ★

29  Sunday

# Thomas Carlyle

## SUSAN EILENBERG

Is the better response to such a man to erect a statue or to hurl rotten eggs? It is discomfiting to find oneself responding on such a level to a sage whose writing, filled with a passionate concern for the (white, male) working poor (and contempt, it sometimes seems, for nearly everyone else), set the terms in which Victorian Britain debated its social and moral state. It is even more discomfiting (indifference seeming even now not an option) to find the question, adulation or eggs, hard to decide. But it has always been so. There were, to be sure, those among his contemporaries who rejected him, turning back on him his own favourite vocabulary of derision, abusing him as a quack, a sham, a flunkey, a phantasm, a canting charlatan, a crank 'foaming and gasping, as it were, in one eternal epileptic fit of wonder', all 'barking and froth'. And there were others who heard as prophetic wisdom Carlyle's harangues about the rightness of despotism, the ingratitude of slaves, the desirability of flogging idle paupers and the folly of any particular reform. But many more were ambivalent, unable to reconcile the stirring rhetoric with the often brutal politics or, as Emerson had it, 'the magnificence of his genius & the poverty of his aims'. His ideological allies (there were ever fewer of them as he passed middle age) sometimes felt they were in the presence of a man 'doing the right thing, but kicking you while he does it'.

Vol. 26 No. 19 · 7 October 2004

30  Monday

ST ANDREW'S DAY (SCOT)

1  Tuesday

2  Wednesday

3  Thursday

4  Friday ★

5  Saturday

6  Sunday

# Lucian Freud

## CELIA PAUL

David Dawson, Lucian's long-serving assistant, described Susanna Chancellor, the woman who remained Lucian's partner longer than anyone else, as 'a proper woman, not one of these neurotics'. She is the girlfriend who replaced me.

People don't become artists if they are sane and well-adjusted. The world is indulgent towards the neurotic male artist. The more impossible his behaviour, the more he is valued. The world disapproves of neurosis in a female artist. This disapproval fills her with shame and undermines her confidence. Lucian was attracted to young women artists precisely because they were neurotic. He was drawn to their vulnerability. There is a sad pattern to this biography: the long list of sensitive young women, one after another, who fall for Lucian and, when they become too dependent and needy, are dumped by him. He always encouraged the infatuation, needing their dependence, until he felt too claustrophobic to stand them any longer.

Lucian didn't like to be thought of in connection with other artists. But he was pleased if he was compared to Rodin. He liked to tell me that he had the same birthday, 8 December, as Rodin's lover, the sculptor Camille Claudel, while Suzy Boyt, the mother of four of his children, had the same birthday as Rodin: 12 November. Lucian thought this showed that their relationship had a special significance. My birthday is 11 November.

Vol. 42 No. 24 · 17 December 2020

7 Monday

8 Tuesday ★

9 Wednesday

10 Thursday

11 Friday

12 Saturday

13 Sunday

# Aphra Behn

## MICHAEL DOBSON

We can be fairly confident that Behn was the daughter of a Canterbury barber called Johnson, born on 14 December 1640 and christened Eaffrey. From here onwards, though, things get difficult. When we next hear of her, Eaffrey/Aphra is in her mid-twenties and calling herself Mrs Behn, though of Mr Behn we have only a report in the posthumous and unreliable 'Life and Memoirs of Mrs. Behn' that he was 'a merchant of Dutch extraction'. (Whoever he was, he seems to have vanished entirely, leaving no children behind him, long before Behn had her first play produced.) Before 1666, Johnson/Behn may have visited the English colony at Surinam, the setting for *Oroonoko*, where she may have gathered political intelligence for Charles II's government. During 1666 she certainly undertook such a mission to Antwerp, where she contacted a Cromwellian exile called William Scot, offering him a pardon in exchange for information on alleged Dutch plans to invade England with the help of other banished republicans. (Hence her routine description in literature textbooks as 'playwright and spy'.) After this paradoxically well-documented secret excursion, however (the letters Behn wrote under cover as agent 160, code-named Astrea, constitute the bulk of her surviving correspondence), the life pretty much disappears, and there remain only the traces of a prolific literary career.

Vol. 19 No. 9 · 8 May 1997

14  Monday  ★

15  Tuesday

16  Wednesday

17  Thursday

18  Friday

19  Saturday                          20  Sunday

# Edith Thompson

## SUSANNAH CLAPP

On 3 October 1922 Percy Thompson, a shipping clerk and old member of the Stepney Elocution Class, was stabbed to death in the street near his home in Ilford. His wife, Edith, was with him; her lover and former lodger, Frederick Bywaters, was the attacker. These circumstances were not disputed when the couple were charged with Thompson's murder. But when they were found guilty and sentenced to hang, the clamour for reprieve was insistent. The magistrate who had committed them for trial at the Old Bailey protested to the Home Office. The *Daily Sketch* featured front-page pictures of the lovers' parents. A petition seeking commutation of the sentence, placed in cinemas, tube stations and theatres, was signed by over a million people.

No one thought that Edith Thompson had actually stabbed her husband; many people thought that she had meant to seduce Bywaters into doing so. 'Illicit love may lead to crime,' the judge instructed the jury, adding unconvincingly: 'You must not, of course, let your disgust carry you too far.' In her novel about the case, *A Pin to See the Peepshow*, F. Tennyson Jesse suggested that the crime for which Edith Thompson was really tried was adultery, and that it was disgust at her love affair with a younger man which condemned her. Tennyson Jesse did not say that Thompson was blameless: she did say that she shouldn't have been hanged, and wouldn't have been had she been a man.

Vol. 10 No. 14 · 4 August 1988

21 Monday

22 Tuesday

23 Wednesday

24 Thursday

25 Friday ★                                    CHRISTMAS DAY

26 Saturday                          27 Sunday

# J.R.R. Tolkien

## JENNY TURNER

Look at him as he sits there in photographs, with his pipe and his tweedy jacket. What shattering sorrows that figure is struggling to contain. He lost his father, his mother, his childhood really. The war took from him his friends, his idealism, a good proportion of his self-belief. And yet, he kept on going. His letters show a man of loyalty, generosity and lovely manners (though not much irony or sense of the ridiculous, and he does complain a lot about being ill). The letters he wrote to his sons are demonstrative and tender. 'God bless you, my dear son. I pray for you constantly,' he writes to his first-born, Michael, in 1941. 'My dearest,' he addresses his younger son, Christopher.

What else can we learn from Tolkien's letters? Well, he loved trees and the English countryside, and hated cars and machinery. He hated France and the French, although he did like Venice: 'elvishly lovely', he said. He loathed 'that ruddy little ignoramus Adolf Hitler', which will come as a relief to readers worried about the Nordic connection. And this is what he wrote to Stanley Unwin after a German publisher asked him to make a declaration of Aryan extraction in 1938: 'I do not regard the (probable) absence of Jewish blood as necessarily honourable; and I have many Jewish friends, and should regret giving any colour to the notion that I subscribe to the wholly pernicious and unscientific race-doctrine'.

Vol. 23 No. 22 · 15 November 2001

28 Monday

29 Tuesday

30 Wednesday

31 Thursday

1 Friday

NEW YEAR'S DAY

2 Saturday

3 Sunday ★

# Ignatius Sancho

## SUKHDEV SANDHU

Sancho was born in 1729 on board a slave ship sailing to the Spanish West Indies. His mother soon fell sick and died; his father committed suicide. At the age of two he was brought to Greenwich and looked after by three sisters, who gave him the surname 'Sancho', thinking he looked like Cervantes's comic anti-hero. Sancho was fortunate to find a patron in John, 2nd Duke of Montagu, who lived nearby in Blackheath, and had been known to rescue from penury complete strangers he found wandering in St James's Park. Against the wishes of the sisters, the duke insisted on helping Sancho learn about music and literature, and to this end presented the young African with gifts of books. Yet this was the same man who planned a seaport and depot near his family home in Beaulieu Creek in order to profit from the slave trade. When the duke died, Sancho received £70 plus a £30 annuity. He headed for the capital, where he lived the life of a libertine and gambled excessively, on one occasion losing all his clothes in a game of cribbage. Inevitably, he soon went back to being a servant in the Montagu household.

His letters are, by turns, funny, sententious, moralistic. They contain perspicacious literary criticism, topical verse, funny descriptions of being stuck in stagecoaches with fat, farting and loud-mouthed white couples, as well as unique vignettes of black family life in the 18th century, and a very vivid account of the Gordon Riots.

Vol. 19 No. 4 · 20 February 1997

4 Monday

5 Tuesday

6 Wednesday

7 Thursday

8 Friday

9 Saturday

10 Sunday

# Francis Williams

## FARA DABHOIWALA

The portrait of Francis Williams is the only painting ever made of Halley's comet in 1759, on its momentous first predicted return. It was an event with huge significance for Williams – and for every other intellectual across the Enlightenment world. It marked the triumph of Newtonian science, of a new, rational scientific and religious outlook. A triumph of British scientists. A triumph of scholars from Cambridge. To all those overlapping, Enlightened worlds, Williams's painting conveys a proud visual message: 'I, Francis Williams, free Black gentleman and scholar, born in Jamaica and educated in Britain, witnessed the return of Halley's comet – and I calculated its exact trajectory, according to the rules of the third edition of Isaac Newton's *Principia*.'

On the table, dipped in ink, are the mathematical instruments with which he has done this; behind him is the comet. It is a work of breathtaking intellectual poise and self-confidence. It shows a Black person, born to enslaved African parents, who already as a youth was mathematically talented enough to understand the most complicated, avant-garde science in the world. As a young man he engaged with the brilliant creators of the new, Newtonian principles of the Enlightenment. At the end of his life, aged almost seventy, he celebrated that they had been proved right, and associated himself with that achievement – the greatest revolution in science before the 20th century.

Vol. 46 No. 22 · 21 November 2024

11 Monday

12 Tuesday

13 Wednesday

14 Thursday

15 Friday

16 Saturday

17 Sunday

**NOTES**

# NOTES

# About the *London Review of Books*

The *London Review of Books* is Europe's leading magazine of culture and ideas, published twice a month. It provides the space for many of the world's best writers to explore a wide variety of subjects in exhilarating detail – from art and politics to science and technology via history and philosophy, fiction and poetry. In the age of the long read, the *LRB* remains the pre-eminent exponent of the intellectual essay, admired around the world for its fearlessness, its range and its elegance.

As well as book reviews and reportage, each issue also contains poems, reviews of exhibitions and movies, 'short cuts', letters and a diary, and is available in print, online, and offline via our app. Subscribers enjoy unlimited online access to our archive, which includes every piece we've published since 1979, the year the magazine was founded. On lrb.co.uk you'll also find a regular blog, weekly podcasts and occasional documentaries, and the latest news of events, publications, products, partnerships and special projects from the magazine, the London Review Bookshop, and the LRB Store.

A reader recently described the *LRB* as 'the best thing about being a human'. Make it a highlight of your fortnight, too, by subscribing: lrb.me/sub

# More LRB Books

London Review of Books: An Incomplete History (Faber)

Mantel Pieces: Royal Bodies and Other Writing from the
London Review of Books by Hilary Mantel (4th Estate)

A Hitch in Time: Writings from the London Review of Books
by Christopher Hitchens (Atlantic Books)

The Family Plot: Three Pieces about Containment
by Clair Wills

Extractive Capitalism: How Commodities and Cronyism Drive
the Global Economy by Laleh Khalili (Profile Books)

### COLLECTIONS

1. Royal Bodies: Writing about the Windsors
2. Foodists: Writing about Eating
3. The Flood: Writing about Rising Seas
4. Four in a Bed: Writing about Sex
5. Sinomania: Writing about China
6. Frock Consciousness: Writing about Clothes
7. Broom, Broom: Writing about Witches
8. The Meaninglessness of Meaning: Writing about the Theory Wars
9. Anyone for gulli-danda? Writing about Sport
10. Why Goldwyn Wore Jodhpurs: Writing about Hollywood
11. That Year Again: Writing about 1922
12. Sisters Come Second: Writing about Siblings

### SELECTIONS

1. Frank Kermode
2. Penelope Fitzgerald
3. Barbara Everett

Find them all at the London Review Bookshop,
or online: lrb.me/morebooks